I0605192

POLITICAL SYSTEMS IN ACTION

COMMUNISM

From Marxism to North Korea

ALEX WEBB

Published in 2025 by **Cheriton Children's Books**
1 Bank Drive West, Shrewsbury, Shropshire, SY3 9DJ, UK

First Edition

Author: Alex Webb
Designer: Paul Myerscough
Editor: Sarah Eason
Proofreader: Anna Chambers

Picture credits: Cover: Doodle Press. Inside: p4: Shutterstock/Fourb, p5: Shutterstock/Astrelok, p6: Shutterstock/MehmetO, p9: Shutterstock/Everett Collection, p10: Shutterstock/Alexey Borodin, p11: Shutterstock/Zbynek Burival, p12: Shutterstock/Hung Chung Chih, p13: Shutterstock/Hung Chung Chih, p14: Shutterstock/Jorisvo, p15: U.S. National Archives and Records Administration, p16: Shutterstock/Oleg Golovnev, p17: Shutterstock/All Themes, p19: Shutterstock/Alexander Khitrov, p20: Shutterstock/BAZA Production, p21: Shutterstock/Sasa Dzambic Photography, p22: Shutterstock/Testing, p25: Shutterstock/LMspencer, p26: Shutterstock/SL Chen, p27: Wikimedia Commons/Re:publica, p28: Wikimedia Commons/U.S. Mission Geneva/Eric Bridiers, p29: Shutterstock/Gregory Stein, p30: Shutterstock/Oleg Znamenskiy, p31: Shutterstock/Chriss73, p33: Shutterstock/Yandry KW, p34: Shutterstock/Dmytro Gilitukha, p35: Shutterstock/Yandry KW, p37: Alamy/Associated Press, p38: Alamy/Newscom, p39: Wikimedia Commons/The White House, p40: Shutterstock/Sorbis, p41: Shutterstock/SPhotograph, p42: Shutterstock/Galyna Andrushko, p43: Shutterstock/Kateko, p44: Shutterstock/Twinsterphoto, p45: Shutterstock/Attila Jandi.

Printed in the United States of America

Contents

CHAPTER 1

The Story of Communism

The communist system began as an ideal—it was a way to share the wealth created in a country and eliminate social classes. It arose in the mid-1800s and was adopted by many countries in the 1900s. Although few countries are communist today, it is the system of government in the country with the most people in the world—China. Communism is a distinct form of government and can be considered the opposite of capitalism.

Sharing the Wealth

The communist ideal is to create a society without social classes and to equally share the wealth of a country. A social class is a group of people who share the same economic status. In a society with classes, people can be grouped into upper, middle, working, and poor classes. The upper classes are wealthy and may control businesses and land, and have power and influence. Lower classes have less money and influence, and struggle more to obtain the basic necessities of life.

This old communist poster from China represents the ideal that all citizens are equal, under a strong leader.

The system of communism is in place in North Korea, Asia. This photograph shows a military parade in the country, where past communist leaders are commemorated as eternal leaders of the people.

For the Benefit of the Group

In a communist society, the government controls the economy, and there is only one political party. There is no private ownership of land or capital. In theory, everything becomes public and is shared for the benefit of the group, rather than solely the benefit of the individual.

Just One Party

In many countries, there are several political parties, each representing different values and views for the country. Voters choose the party candidates they favor in an election. In a communist system, voters are offered just one party—the communist party. Elections may be held, but the candidates will only belong to the communist party.

COMMUNISM: PAST AND PRESENT

In this book we will look at the political system of communism, its history, and its place in the world today. We'll compare communism past with communism present, and look at some of the key figures of this political system in the People and Politics features. Look out too for the Communism in Action features throughout the book and try to answer the questions that accompany some of these features.

An Ancient Start

The idea of a society in which goods are shared equally has been around since the fourth century BCE. The ancient Greek philosopher Plato wrote about the concept of an equal society in his book *The Republic*. He believed that when individuals owned goods, it made them selfish.

Plato thought that there should be a group of guardians who ensured goods were shared among people. Plato believed that all people should contribute what they could to the group for the benefit of all within it.

This statue shows Karl Marx (1818–1883) and Friedrich Engels (1820–1895). These two men are credited with creating the communist system (see opposite).

The Industrial Revolution

In the Industrial Revolution of the nineteenth century, a large working class arose. This was a time when new machinery, fuels, building materials, and work systems were developed, which made it possible to create large quantities of goods quickly and cheaply in factories. People moved to growing cities to work in those factories, becoming the working class. The owners of big businesses grew wealthy, but the working class did not make a lot of money, worked long hours with few breaks, and lived in poor conditions.

Karl Marx and Big Changes

German philosopher Karl Marx noticed the evolving class differences and believed European society was corrupt. He thought it could not be fixed and had to change. He joined with his friend Friedrich Engels, another German philosopher, to write a pamphlet criticizing capitalism and outlining a new type of society—a communist society. This pamphlet, *The Communist Manifesto* (originally *Manifesto of the Communist Party*), was published in 1848. It called upon the working class to unite and fight against the capitalist system and those in charge. Marx's theory, called Marxism, also explained how revolutions could be used to overthrow capitalism and replace it with communism.

Communism in Action

The following quote is from the final section of *The Communist Manifesto*.

> "In short, the communists everywhere support every revolutionary movement against the existing social and political order of things. The communists ... openly declare that their ends can be attained only by the forcible overthrow of all existing social conditions. Let the ruling classes tremble at a communistic revolution."

PAST AND PRESENT:

The ruling classes that Marx and Engels wrote about were the elite upper classes of the time—people who had often inherited their position and wealth. Who do you think the ruling classes might be if Marx and Engels were commenting on society today?

How do you think others interpreted Marx and Engels' message in *The Communist Manifesto* at the time it was published?

Revolution or Peace

Marx died in 1883, but Engels continued with his work. After the death of Engels in 1895, Marxist followers split into two groups. One group believed that the transition to communism should be peaceful and happen gradually, the other believed revolution was necessary to make the changes that were required.

Uprising Without Debate

Vladimir Lenin (1870–1924) was a political leader in Russia in the early twentieth century. His party, the Russian Social-Democratic Workers' Party, believed that the best way to achieve communism was through revolution. Most people in Russia at the time were poor peasant farmers who worked land owned by wealthy nobles, and they were unhappy with the system of government. Lenin believed that the country was ready for a revolution, led by a ruling party made up of knowledgeable people, or intellectuals, like himself, who would decide on a direction for the good of the people. The people would not be able to debate or change that direction, which meant that the party would have to enforce strict rules that everyone would have to follow.

Riots in Russia

In 1917, the leader of Russia was Tsar Nicholas II, a monarch whose father had been the previous leader. The people were not happy because Russia had lost many soldiers during World War I (1914–1918) and because of food shortages in the country. Riots broke out, the tsar was forced to step down, and the Russian parliament appointed a temporary government to control the country.

The Communists Step In

However, another party soon took over—the communists, who were led by Lenin. They called themselves the Bolsheviks, meaning "the majority." This new government seized control of the country's industries and land owned by the nobles, and then gave that land to the peasants. Russia had become the first communist country, and was formed into the Union of Soviet Socialist Republics (USSR).

The hammer and sickle is a communist symbol representing unity between industrial workers and peasants, or poor people who farmed the land.

For centuries, tsars such as Nicholas II had total power over Russia. They did not necessarily know how to run a country, but made decisions that affected all of Russia's people. The tsars and their families had lavish lifestyles, wore furs and jewels, and lived in extravagant palaces. Tsar Nicholas II reigned from 1894 and was the last tsar of Russia. He abdicated in 1917 during the Russian Revolution, bringing an end to the Romanov dynasty that had ruled Russia for more than 300 years. The following year, Nicholas, his wife Alexandra, and their five children were killed by the Bolsheviks.

A Power Struggle

Lenin ruled Russia until his death in 1924. This left three other Bolshevik leaders—Joseph Stalin, Leon Trotsky, and Nikolay Bukharin—in power. Stalin wanted to be the sole leader of the USSR, so he had Trotsky and Bukharin removed from power. He then sent millions of people he claimed to be spies or against the party to prison, or to labor camps in a remote and desolate region called Siberia, and had thousands of people executed. Stalin gained control and introduced his own form of communism—Stalinism.

The Cult of Stalin

Under Stalin, communism was changed to fit his needs. He thought a communist leader should be able to do whatever he thought was best, even if it went against communist ideals. Stalin also said that the communist party was filled with traitors and that the power needed to rest on one supreme leader—himself. Stalin developed a cult of personality, using media, control, and propaganda to build a presence about himself as an absolute ruler, almost like a king. His cult of personality helped him maintain an iron grip on the USSR.

A poster of Joseph Stalin (1878–1953) is held aloft, as Russians gather to commemorate the centenary of the Russian Revolution, when the Bolsheviks came to power.

Hidden Behind the Iron Curtain

After World War II, Stalin set up communist systems in other eastern European countries, including Czechoslovakia, Poland, Hungary, Yugoslavia, Romania, Albania, and East Germany. These communist countries created a geographical divider between the USSR and central and western Europe. This barrier, called the Iron Curtain, separated communist and noncommunist countries. Behind the Iron Curtain, the USSR became totally isolated from the international community.

The remains of the Iron Curtain in the Czech Republic, which was a heavily guarded border between East and West.

Communism in Action

Sir Winston Churchill (1874–1965) was the prime minister of the United Kingdom (UK) from 1940 to 1945. In one of his famous speeches, he coined the term "Iron Curtain." Here is an excerpt from that speech:

> "From Stettin in the Baltic to Trieste in the Adriatic, an iron curtain has descended across the Continent. … The Communist parties, which were very small in all these Eastern States of Europe, have been raised to pre-eminence and power far beyond their numbers and are seeking everywhere to obtain [total] control."

What do Churchill's words tell you about the term "Iron Curtain"?

PAST AND PRESENT:

Do you think Russia is still hidden behind an Iron Curtain? Give reasons for your answers.

Communism Takes Hold in China

While communism was growing in the USSR, it was also developing in China. The Chinese Communist Party took control of the government in 1949. Its leader was Mao Zedong, who developed his own form of communism, called Maoism. Unlike communism in the USSR, Maoism focused more on the rural peasants than the urban workers. At the time in China, there were hundreds of millions of peasants living in poverty, and Mao believed that they were the revolutionary force that could overthrow the government. This peasant force was the basis for Mao's communist rule.

A Leap Forward?

Mao's belief in the power of this force led to a plan, called the Great Leap Forward, to speed up China's industry. The plan, which lasted from 1958 to 1960, encouraged peasants to form communities, called "collectives," to produce steel in local backyard furnaces. This effort turned into a national disaster, disrupting agriculture and causing less food to be produced. As a result, around 20 million Chinese people starved to death between 1959 and 1962.

This monument in Tiananmen Square, Beijing, commemorates the workers under their leader, Mao.

Child against Parent

In 1966, Mao launched a new campaign, the Cultural Revolution. He wanted to promote the values of peasant life, while removing the influence of intellectuals and the elite, and so urged the youth of China to rid their country of foreign cultural elements. As a result, children turned their parents in to the police for being against Mao. People thought to be traitors were killed or jailed, urban teens were ordered to move to rural areas to work on farms, and literature and music from Western countries were banned to all people.

A New Chinese Culture

A new culture was installed, which included Chinese revolutionary songs and poems, and new art and opera. This created a cult of personality around Mao, who led the country until his death in 1976. China is still under communist rule today.

PEOPLE AND POLITICS

As a young man, Mao Zedong (1893–1976), fought in a revolution that saw the abdication of the last emperor of China in 1912. He became interested in communism at university and joined the Communist Party of China (CPC) in 1921, later becoming the party's leader in 1935. After a bitter civil war with the anticommunist Nationalist Party, the CPC emerged victorious and created the Republic of China in 1949. Mao would be China's leader until his death in 1976, at the age of 82.

Mao Zedong

Communism Today

Communism reached its peak in the twentieth century, when nearly one-third of the world's people lived in communist countries. The USSR collapsed in 1991, bringing an end to communism there, and today only five countries are under communist rule—China, Cuba, Vietnam, Laos, and North Korea. All, except North Korea, have made moves toward capitalism, allowing at least some economic competition.

Communism in North Korea

The communist party came to power in North Korea in 1946. When its first leader, Kim Il-sung, died in 1994, his son, Kim Jong-il, took control. When he died in 2011, his son, Kim Jong-un, became leader. The Kim family has controlled North Korea for more than 75 years. North Korea is the only country in the world that still follows the strict USSR style of communism.

Communism in Cuba

The small Latin American island of Cuba became communist in 1959, when a revolutionary leader named Fidel Castro led a rebel army that overthrew the Cuban government. Fidel Castro remained president of the country until 2006, when his brother, Raul Castro, took over.

Communism in Vietnam and Laos

In 1954, the southeast Asian country of Vietnam split into North Vietnam and South Vietnam. The north became communist under the leadership of Ho Chi Minh (1890–1969), while the south was anticommunist. The United States fought to keep communism out of the south, but failed and in 1975, North Vietnam took control of the south, uniting the country under communist rule. Next to Vietnam is the country of Laos. It became communist in 1975, establishing a similar type of rule to that of Vietnam. Laos's communist government replaced a monarchy that had ruled for 600 years.

A portrait of Vietnam's former president, communist leader Ho Chi Minh.

Communism in Action

From 1965 to 1973, the United States fought in Vietnam to try and stop the spread of communism. The war had deadly effects, with around 200,000–250,000 South Vietnamese soldiers and 58,000 US soldiers killed. The fighting took place mostly in the thick rain forest of Vietnam, where the communist soldiers knew how to move and hide better than the US soldiers. Eventually, the United States withdrew and Vietnam became communist.

Why do you think the United States government feared communism taking hold in Vietnam?

PAST AND PRESENT:

Can you imagine a scenario in which the United States intervenes to stop the spread of communism today? Where in the world do you think such an intervention might take place if it were to occur?

Many US soldiers would never recover from their experiences in the Vietnam War.

CHAPTER 2

The System of Communism

In their *Manifesto*, Marx and Engels outlined a plan to set up a communist government in a country. The plan became the basis for all communist movements around the world. Marx and Engels believed that there were two main classes of people in modern capitalist society—the bourgeoisie and the proletariat. The plan centered on radically changing the status quo of those two classes and creating a new system of control.

Upper and Lower

The bourgeoisie were the upper class. They had political power, made political decisions that benefited their class, and controlled much of the land and the production of goods. The proletariat were the modern working class of people, who labored in factories, basically helping machines do the work needed to produce goods. They were paid just enough to live, but not enough to have a decent life. However, Marx and Engels believed in the strength of this class once its people were united, and thought that they were the people who could cause change in the political system. The communist party aligned with the working-class people, choosing to represent the needs of the proletariat.

This nineteenth century engraving shows a shoe factory in St Petersburg, Russia, where the work of the proletariat benefited the bourgeoisie.

Communism in Action

The communist flag emerged during the Russian Revolution. The hammer and sickle represent the industrial and agricultural workers of the proletariat.

A New Order

According to Marx and Engels, capitalist society could not be fixed. It had to be overthrown and replaced with a communist structure, which would ideally focus on the needs of the masses, rather than of the ruling few. However, for that new structure to take hold, revolution had to take place. This meant that the proletariat would have to join and take control of the government by force. Once in power, the proletariat would then install a communist regime.

In their *Manifesto*, Marx and Engels outlined the ten basic measures that would have to take place after a revolution. They included the ideas that all land should be publicly owned, the government should control all banks and most factories, and that education should be free for all children in public schools.

Do you think *The Communist Manifesto* suggested major or minor changes?

Do you think it was easy or difficult for people to give up their land to the government after it became communist?

PAST AND PRESENT:

Can you imagine a scenario in which a similar revolution could happen today in a country that is not currently communist? What conditions would need to be in place for that to occur?

One Type of Economy

Different communist countries operate in different ways, but they all have a type of economic system called a "command economy," which is very different from the market economy in the United States. In a market economy, the production of goods is based on what consumers need. The consumers buy what they need, which then lets the suppliers know what goods are required, how quickly, and at what price they can be sold. In a command economy, the government tells suppliers what and how many goods they need to make, and what prices suppliers can charge for goods.

Controlling Everything

In a communist country, the government controls the production of all goods and sets production goals for industries. The government also controls the amount of raw materials each supplier can have in order to produce the amount of goods needed to reach their goals.

In theory, the practice of controlling production leads to a more efficient use of natural resources. It should also help the government provide, when needed, a large amount of goods in a short time. However, consumers have limited choices of goods, and the country may also experience shortages of certain goods if demands are higher than the country's set production goals.

Communism in Action

The USSR's command economy caused major shortages of food and goods. North Korea still follows the Soviet-style command economy, and its people have experienced many food shortages as a result. China, Cuba, and Vietnam have all made changes toward market economies.

Why do you think North Korea still follows the Soviet-style command economy, despite the hardship it causes people?

Why do you think North Korea's leader believes that the policy of command economy is acceptable? What does this tell you about his views and leadership approach?

PAST AND PRESENT:

Why do you think China, Cuba, and Vietnam all changed their economic policies? What do you think might happen in those countries if a command economy was imposed there today?

Kim Jong-un

When Kim Jong-il died in 2011, his youngest son Kim Jong-un became one of the world's youngest leaders at the age of 27. Kim Jong-un's older brothers had fallen out of favor with the family, or were thought unsuitable to govern.

Kim Jong-un has enormous personal wealth. North Korea's controversial leader owns several spectacular palaces, in which he lives with his wife and children.

The Power of Media

The media, which includes newspapers, television, the Internet, and now social media, is a powerful tool. The media can be used to spread information and persuade the public about different ideas. Communist countries control the media and stop information that they believe may be used against the government. Many communist governments also spread the party's message to the people of the country by saying positive things about themselves, and negative things about their enemies, including lies. This is called "propaganda."

Controlling the Press

The press, such as newspapers and magazines, is tightly controlled in communist countries. Certain stories may be edited or completely banned by people, called censors, who check all areas of the media. According to the Worldwide Press Freedom Index (WPFI) of 2023, communist countries rank low in terms of press freedom. Of the 180 countries in the list, North Korea was at 180, China 179, Vietnam 178, Cuba 172, and Laos 160. In comparison, the press in Norway, Ireland, and Denmark—all democratic countries—had the most freedom.

Freedom of the press is vital in a democracy to give voters informed opinions.

The Danger of Free Speech

Journalists in communist countries have often been arrested and jailed for writing stories that were critical of the government, or that included information the government did not want to be released. For example, Reporters Without Borders, an organization that was set up to protect journalists, reported that more than 100 journalists were imprisoned in China in 2023.

Powerful Messages

A poster, a statue, a song, or even a poem can be a piece of propaganda. What all propaganda contains is a message that promotes a certain political view. Sometimes, these messages come in the form of a slogan. Many times, propaganda spreads false information. All communist countries use some form of political propaganda to try and convince people and control opinion. Lenin, the first leader of the USSR, used the following slogan as propaganda: "The dictatorship of the proletariat will bring us from capitalism's gloom and oppression to a radiant future [under communism]."

PEOPLE AND POLITICS

Over the past 25 years, Vladimir Putin has taken a firm grip on the media in Russia to legitimize his leadership. Some newspapers have been forced to shut down, and hundreds of journalists have been arrested or even killed. Many independent television channels have been banned, and Internet sites and social media platforms have been blocked too.

President Putin

A Lifetime in Power

In a communist country, the communist party controls all aspects of the government. The leader of the communist party is also the chief executive of the country's government. Typically, there is no term limit for this leader. This person can serve for a lifetime, as many communist leaders, such as Mao Zedong and Kim Il-sung, have. While each communist government around the world has its differences, most have a similar structure.

Making Decisions

China's communist government is structured in a particular way. Although the leader has the final decision, issues are first discussed within a group of advisors. In China, this group is called the politburo, which has up to 25 members. The members of the politburo debate an issue and then make their decision about how to act. This decision then becomes a policy, and the politburo members are bound to that policy.

The National People's Congress (NPC) meets in the Great Hall of the People in Beijing.

The Law-Making Group

The legislature, or law-making body, in China is the NPC. It is a parliament with almost 3,000 members. This large group does not do much of the work, however. A select committee of about 150 members does. In theory, the legislature has the power to change the constitution and make laws. In reality, it gives its official stamp to policies decided by the leader and politburo. Smaller local legislatures deal with local issues.

A Five-Year Plan

The task of the State Council is to make sure that the government carries out the communist party's decisions. This department drafts the country's economic plans and budgets, setting five-year plans for the country's economic course. In 2021, China released its fourteenth five-year plan. The plan has a range of social and economic goals. One of the most important was to rapidly strengthen China's economy, which had been significantly damaged by various lockdowns put in place during the COVID-19 pandemic.

Communism in Action

In China, elections are held for legislative representatives at local levels. However, most people do not take the legislature seriously, believing it has no real power. Candidates only belong to the communist party and are approved by the party. Voters do not have much of a choice, but are required to vote.

After reading about Chinese elections, compare what you have learned with what you know about US elections. How are Chinese elections similar or different?

How do you think American citizens would react if they were told that they could vote only for candidates from one party?

What might the reaction in China be if its citizens were told they had a choice of candidates from different parties?

The Cult of Personality

For many communist leaders, having a cult of personality helps control the public. This is an idealized public image developed using media, propaganda, and, sometimes, false information. The leader becomes an almost godlike figure that can say or do things with little public doubt or questioning. In many instances, opposition to them is met by imprisonment or death. The cult of personality is an especially helpful position for a dictator to hold. Several communist leaders have been known for their larger-than-life cult of personality. One of them is Mao Zedong.

Bigger and Bigger

During the Cultural Revolution, Mao Zedong's personality cult grew. His image and slogans could be seen everywhere, from the pins that people wore and his "Little Red Book" of sayings to large murals in public spaces. Images showed Mao holding babies or standing in front of large amounts of food, and included sayings such as "Turn China into a prosperous, rich, and powerful industrialized socialist country under the leadership of the Communist Party and Chairman Mao!" Even children's toys and books contained messages about Mao Zedong and communism.

Communism in Action

The Red Guards were a group of young and passionate communists during the time of the Cultural Revolution. They carried a copy of the "Little Red Book" wherever they went. Here is an excerpt from it:

> "Our duty is to hold ourselves responsible to the people. Every word, every act, and every policy must conform to the people's interests, and if mistakes occur, they must be corrected—that is what being responsible to the people means."

Think about how Mao's words helped his cult of personality. Why do you think this quote was included in the "Little Red Book"?

PAST AND PRESENT:

Do you think that the communist regime in control in China today follows the guidance of the "Little Red Book" excerpt above? Give reasons for your answer.

PEOPLE AND POLITICS

The communist government of North Korea strictly controls its people. That is why a cult of personality is so important to its leaders. The country's one television channel has programs showing the leader Kim Jong-un as a kind of rock star, who is chased by his fans. Huge portraits of the late leaders Kim Il-sung (1912–1994) and Kim Jong-il (1941–2011) tower over public squares. Having a strong cult of personality has helped the Kim family stay in power for decades. The personality cult began soon after Kim Il-sung took power in 1948, and was expanded even further after the leader's death in 1994.

In North Korea, statues of past leaders Kim Il-sung and Kim Jong-il dominate public squares.

CHAPTER 3

Living with Communism

In a democratic society, people enjoy many freedoms. They have free speech, a free press, and the right to protest. They can freely use the Internet and read news from other countries. All of these are accepted and, often, taken-for-granted freedoms. However, life in a communist country is very different, with many freedoms restricted and information controlled. These tight controls are part of daily life in a communist country.

The Spread of Misinformation

It was easier to control information before the Internet evolved, which allows information to be quickly spread around the world. What worries communist governments is that their country's people may read or spread information that criticizes or undermines the government. To combat this spread of information, China has developed an Internet-filtering system that controls who has access to the Internet and what content can be accessed. For example, searching for "democracy movements" will lead to a blank screen that states, "page cannot be displayed." North Korea completely bans the public from going online.

Jack Ma founded one of the world's largest e-commerce businesses, Alibaba, but his work is closely monitored by the Chinese government.

Ban on Blogging

Blogging is also restricted in communist countries, although some journalists have found ways around this. One famous Cuban blogger, Yoani Sánchez, started 14ymedio in 2014. It is an online news service, which uploads content using the Wi-Fi at hotels. In China, the government simply shuts down blogs if they believe the posted messages are at all inappropriate.

Yoani Sánchez's news service covers political and economic developments as well as social and cultural activities. The blogger has been named one the World's 100 Most Influential People by *Time Magazine*.

Communism in Action

Modern artist Ai Weiwei uses social media and art to protest against the Chinese political system and stand up for human rights in his country. On X, he voices his thoughts about censorship and freedom, and his art makes statements about issues in China. Through X, Weiwei escapes the censorship enforced by the government on other forms of media. Weiwei has said of X (formerly Twitter):

> "Twitter is my city, my favorite city. I can talk to anybody I want to. And anybody who wants to talk to me will get my response. They know me better than their relatives or my relatives."

After reading about Weiwei, what do you think this quote means?

The Price of Speaking Out

Speaking out in a communist country is a risk. Many journalists have been jailed for reporting news the government did not want to be released, and police have detained bloggers and activists without being charged. Sometimes, people are sent to harsh prison camps. The police rarely help people. Many are corrupt, and accept bribes and use violence to get people to do as they wish.

During the twentieth and twenty-first centuries, there have been numerous accounts of murders, deportations, disappearances, and wrongful imprisonments in communist countries around the world. Ordinary people are therefore very fearful of speaking out against governments in countries that carry out such actions.

A Network of Prisons

North Korea has a large network of prison camps, with perhaps as many as 200,000 people jailed in them. Little is known about the camps, except through the few accounts from people who have escaped. The North Korean government denies that the camps even exist.

PEOPLE AND POLITICS

One North Korean escapee from a camp is Shin Dong-hyuk. Shin was born inside a camp and lived within it for 23 years before escaping. He told the television news program *60 Minutes* how prisoners are treated inside the camp. They are beaten and tortured, and many starve to death. After Shin accidentally broke a machine in a factory, the tip of his finger was cut off as a punishment for his action.

Shin Dong-hyuk

Alexei Navalny (1976–2024) was recognized by Amnesty International, the human rights organization, for his work in Russia.

Seeking the Truth

Alexei Navalny was a Russian lawyer, politician, and activist who became one of the most famous critics of President Putin. He was jailed several times for criticizing the Russian regime, but despite the dangers he faced the journalist remained defiant in his fight against corruption. In 2020, Navalny became seriously sick while campaigning ahead of regional elections. Tests revealed that he had been poisoned. Navalny survived this assassination attempt—an example of efforts to silence Putin's critics—but in 2024, it was announced that the journalist had died in custody, at the age of 47.

Communism in Action

In a 2022 documentary about the work of Alexei Navalny, the political activist referred to the assassination attempt that nearly took his life.

> "If they decide to kill me, it means that we are incredibly strong. We need to utilize this power to not give up, to remember that we are a huge power that is being oppressed."

What do you think Navalny meant about being incredibly strong? Why did he feel it was important to say these words in the event of his death?

In a democracy, how are critics of the government treated? Why might it be important to see and hear both sides of a story?

Going Without

Because of the command economies in communist countries, shortages are common. If the production of goods does not meet the need for those goods, shortages occur, and people may wait for hours in long lines to get a loaf of bread or piece of meat. The government often rations the supplies to make them last longer, but the people may then lack enough food to feed their families.

A Nation of Children Suffer

Many North Korean children suffer from malnutrition because of food shortages. According to a United Nations (UN) report in 2022, more than 40 percent of North Koreans were undernourished. Food insecurity in the country has worsened because of failed harvests, international sanctions, and severe lockdowns during the COVID-19 pandemic. Fuel and equipment shortages affect food production in the country as well. Without tractors that work, farmers are unable to plant and harvest crops to feed the country's 26 million people.

The Cost in Cuba

In Cuba, food shortages make the price of food rise higher, and that causes the prices of other goods to also rise. Fuel and medical supplies are also in short supply. With a lack of food production at home, Cuba currently imports around 70 percent of its food requirements and this is growing increasingly expensive.

Turning to the Black Market

People in communist countries must sometimes buy goods from the black market to meet their needs. A black market is an illegal system of trade in which goods may be sold at very high prices. In communist countries with shortages, those with the money can supplement their basic food supply with goods from the black market.

Children in North Korea face many challenges from lack of food to lack of education.

Cuban citizens wait at a store to buy some food in 2022, amid growing food shortages.

Communism in Action

In North Korea, a thriving black market has been the only means of survival for some. Reports claim around one-fifth of the population depend on this form of trading. Markets have developed selling street food, clothes, and electronic goods smuggled in from China or stolen from the military. Sometimes, the government turns a blind eye (if vendors pay the government for the privilege), while other forms of trade have been restricted. In 2024, new laws prohibited the sale of goods that hadn't been handmade, leading to night-time street vendors trying to shirk the law.

Why do you think the government sometimes turns a blind eye to the black market in North Korea? What might happen if they tried to restrict it further?

Communism and Healthcare

In China, the healthcare system has improved greatly since the 1980s and 1990s. The system was reformed after 2009, with the aim of providing universal health insurance for China's citizens and improved health service efficiency, but high-quality services were mainly confined to the cities. With the impact of the COVID-19 pandemic and rising costs, however, fewer medicines and procedures are now covered by this insurance and citizens are having to pay additional charges. In 2021, 17 million people abandoned the insurance scheme, and numbers are continuing to fall. In communist countries, medical services are either free or mostly covered by the government. However, the quality of these services varies greatly from country to country.

Human Rights in North Korea

In 2010, an investigative report by Amnesty International claimed that North Korea's healthcare system was in a terrible state. Interviews with 40 former North Koreans told of the poor medical care in the country, including the amputation of one man's leg without the use of any anesthesia or pain killers.

Although healthcare is supposed to be free, a worsening economy has meant doctors are poorly paid and medical supplies are scarce. Those who can afford it, pay for the care that they need. Patients must bring money or goods to give doctors or they may not be treated. Those who cannot afford treatment often suffer, without even basic medicine.

Communism in Action

Cuba is an example of a communist country with a strong healthcare system. It can match or beat some of the health statistics found in the United States. Life expectancy in Cuba is almost the same, and its low infant death numbers are similar to those of the United States. Doctors are paid low salaries, but they receive free education and a home.

Do you think there are strategies from the system in Cuba that could be put in place in the United States? If so, which? How might they improve healthcare?

Healthcare in Cuba

In Cuba, healthcare is free and the system is focused on preventing major health problems. Cuba has one of the highest doctor-to-patient ratios in the world and life expectancy is around 74 years of age. Every patient gets a yearly doctor's visit at home and health education is taught in schools. However, the quality of treatment varies. There is little patient choice and resources are limited. Cuba's healthcare has a good reputation but in reality, there is one healthcare for visitors (who pay) and another for citizens (which is free). This is especially true after the challenges of the COVID-19 pandemic, during which massive vaccination was required to try to protect the population from the virus.

Cuban citizens wait at a vaccination center during the COVID-19 pandemic.

Education for All

Free education for all children was one of the key founding principles of communism, as described by Marx and Engels in their *Manifesto.* Education is an important issue in communist countries. Some countries have excellent educational systems and high literacy rates, but there are still costs to students' parents. The government can also use education as a tool to spread its political messages to the people.

Not a Level Playing Field

The Chinese government provides schooling from primary school to attaining a university degree. According to the Central Intelligence Agency (CIA) statistics, the country's current literacy rate is 96.8 percent.

In 2018, students in the Chinese cities of Beijing and Shanghai showed the highest scores in the world in math, science, and reading. However, the standard of education differs between rural and urban schools, with some rural families paying up to half of their small incomes for school transportation or boarding costs.

The Story in Vietnam

Vietnam has a high literacy rate and a large national university. According to the CIA statistics, 95.8 percent of Vietnam's citizens over the age of 15 can read and write. However, some say the country's education system is old-fashioned and is also flawed due to the heavy censorship that is in place in schools and colleges.

Vietnamese children at a rural school. While Vietnam has a high literacy rate, standards vary across the country.

Looking at Cuba

There is a high literacy rate in Cuba. Around 99.7 percent of its population can read and write. Education is free, but the government sets the places available for study each year in the universities. This is related to which industries the government wants to promote. For example, technical and vocational skills have been encouraged, as well as farming to increase the amount of food produced by Cuba to reduce the country's reliance on food imports.

Farmers in Cuba are being encouraged to increase the production of all food crops to try to make this communist country more self-sufficient.

Communism in Action

Youth organizations can be used to spread political messages. During the Cultural Revolution in China, as many as 11 million students joined the Red Guards, which formed when Mao Zedong asked that the youth of the country help find people who were against the regime. Its members accused teachers, intellectuals, and people with traditional Chinese views of being against the government, and many people were killed as a result.

Why do you think the Red Guards was attractive to the Chinese youth?

PAST AND PRESENT: Do you think the youth in China would take on a similar task today if the government instructed them to? Why or why not? Give reasons for your answer.

CHAPTER 4

Fighting against Communism

Although communism was gaining strength in the mid-twentieth century, many democratic countries around the world fought against its spread. People living in communist countries also staged demonstrations against their controlling governments.

Tensions Grow

In the 1940s and 1950s, extreme tension grew between the United States and the USSR, which was known as the Cold War. The United States joined with countries in Europe to form the North Atlantic Treaty Organization (NATO), which was a unified military force against the Soviets. The Cold War continued until the collapse of the USSR in 1991. During the 1960s, Cuba and its close relationship with the USSR posed a nuclear threat to the United States.

Trade and Travel Bans

During the Cuban Missile Crisis in 1962, there was almost a nuclear war between the countries. As a result, the United States blocked all trade with Cuba and travel to the country was banned for decades. In 2000, President Clinton allowed the sale of food and humanitarian products to Cuba, and in 2009 President Obama eased travel restrictions but these were later reinforced by President Trump. In 2024, calls by the UN for the US to lift its trade bans, to help Cuba's economic crisis, were opposed by Israel and the United States, and the bans remain.

The United States trade ban against Cuba prevents all US businesses from carrying out trade with Cuban interests. It is the most long-lasting trade embargo in modern history.

Communism in Action

In the late 1980s, there was a growing anticommunist movement in China, especially among university students. On April 22, 1989, students gathered in Tiananmen Square, a large square in Beijing, to protest for their rights. By mid-May, there were nearly 1 million people demonstrating, so in June, the government responded, sending tanks and armed troops into the square, shooting at the protestors, and killing or wounding many. Thousands were jailed.

Why do you think the government reacted to the Tiananmen Square protestors in this way? Do you think it was right or wrong?

What do you think people around the world felt or thought after seeing the government's reaction on television?

PAST AND PRESENT:

Do you think a similar protest would take place in China today? Why or why not? Give reasons for your answer.

This famous image shows a protestor, who became known as "tank man," standing in front of oncoming tanks in Tiananmen Square in 1989.

PEOPLE AND POLITICS

Liu Xiaobo

People living in communist countries have protested against their governments, but the governments usually quickly stop them, and protesters can be jailed and even executed. One of the most famous Chinese activists was Liu Xiaobo (1955–2017). He participated in the protest in Tiananmen Square in 1989, and wrote a manifesto, called Charter 08, which called for political change in China. Liu was arrested in 2009 for writing the charter, and was then sentenced to 11 years in jail. In 2010, he was awarded the Nobel Peace Prize for his human rights work. He was due to be released in 2020, but died from cancer in 2017.

Secrets and Threats

North Korea is a highly secretive country. It lets little information in to the country, and even less out. However, the messages North Korea does send out are often threats aimed at the United States and South Korea. North Korean propaganda claims the country has far more strength than most people believe it actually does.

Nuclear Danger

The two superpowers—the United States and the USSR—stopped testing nuclear weapons in the 1990s. Testing a nuclear weapon is a way to show the world how much military strength a country has. North Korea has tested nuclear weapons six times between 2006 and 2017—and it has also launched missiles. Some missile tests were failures, but others have succeeded. The country issues frequent threats to the United States and South Korea, stating that it will attack if provoked. The United States does not believe North Korea has the ability to attack. However, the United States also knows North Korea is developing its nuclear weapons.

Hitting Back

Several countries have reacted to the nuclear tests, missile launchings, and threats. The United States, for example, stopped sending food aid to North Korea and imposed laws, called sanctions, to stop people doing business with the country. China has made sanctions against North Korean banking, travel, and trade, and Japan has imposed travel and funding restrictions. The UN has also imposed penalties on the country, banning its nuclear-testing program. The UN also bans trade of weapons and luxury goods, and the transfer of cash along with other types of financial transactions.

Communism in Action

In 2018, Donald Trump became the first sitting US president to meet with a North Korean leader when he met Kim Jong-un in Singapore. Then, a year later, Trump became the first sitting US president to visit North Korea, when he met Kim Jong-un there. These meetings brought hope of a softening of relations, although tensions between the two nations remain high. Despite North Korea's secrecy, Kim Jong-un is keen to build relationships with international leaders. In 2019, he also met with Russia's President Putin for the first time, and there is talk of a future meeting with Japan's prime minister, Fumio Kishida.

A historic meeting took place between Donald Trump and Kim Jong-un in North Korea in 2019.

CHAPTER 5

The Future of Communism

North Korea remains the most Soviet-style communist country in the world. However, other communist countries have made small moves away from communism. China is one of those countries. Communism is also being debated in Vietnam.

The Biggest Exporter

After many economic reforms that began in the 1970s, the economy in China is now labeled as a socialist market economy. There are still some state-owned industries, but many businesses are privately owned. It is very similar to a capitalist economy, and China has become the biggest exporter of goods in the world.

Different Views

Despite (and perhaps because of) China's economic success, the public hold varying views about the way China is ruled. Some wealthier citizens have done well from government policies, while others wish to see more open debate about political issues. Most of China's citizens are patriotic, but they also want to avoid war and conflict. As the country becomes more liberal in its views and a younger generation comes to the fore, it will be interesting to see what direction China takes in its policies and development opportunities.

As China's youth become increasingly wealthy, educated, and well-traveled, it could change their views of their country's system of government.

A Public Debate

In 2013, Vietnam's leaders asked for public comments on their plan to change the country's constitution. What happened instead was a public debate on the communist party's control of the government. The public discussed human rights, land ownership, and wanting an army that was not tied to the communist party. The people also wanted to remove Article 4—an article that guarantees the communist party's government control—from the constitution.

Nguyen Xuan Phuc resigned as president of Vietnam in 2023 after a series of corruption scandals.

Communism in Action

The Vietnamese people were unhappy with their government and the country's economic situation—and the government listened. The revised constitution in 2013 gave greater weight to the basic rights of citizens in modern society, and the protection of human rights. But in practice, the revised constitution didn't change a great deal. Human rights groups say that authorities still block access to websites or social media pages that criticize the government, and anyone who opposes the government faces intimidation or even imprisonment without a fair trial.

What does it take for the principles of a constitution to be upheld?

Why do you think the Vietnamese government made these promises, and why have they been broken?

Economic Worries in the World

Economic troubles also affect the countries of Cuba, Laos, and North Korea. Urgent solutions are needed there to be able to embrace the changing world markets. In December 2012, Cuba's government authorized the creation of nonfarming cooperatives, to allow people to set up small and midsize private businesses. Cuba still had centralized planning of the economy, but it started to open up a little to include these new businesses. But sanctions have hit the country hard, particularly in the wake of the COVID-19 pandemic, which saw a steep decline in Cuba's export earnings, which are needed to buy the imports the country relies on.

Change and New Enterprises

One of the poorest countries in eastern Asia, Laos relies on international donations to survive. Although economic reform in the early part of this century began to embrace some forms of capitalism, there were environmental problems and disputes over land. In 2022, the country suffered a severe economic crisis due to rising prices, a downturn during the COVID-19 pandemic, loss of tourism, and growing debts. Since the crisis, Laos has struggled to recover its economy, with small businesses struggling in particular. The country will need significant support to make a proper recovery.

Laos is a landlocked country but growing poverty means many people rely on the fish in rivers and lakes for food security.

An Iron Grip

In North Korea, Kim Jong-un, like his father and grandfather, has a strong cult of personality. Although there was uncertainty when he came to power at a young age, Jong-un was quick to consolidate his position. He prioritized economic growth and living standards began to improve. He has also focused on improving science and technology. A combination of international sanctions and North Korea's severe lockdown restrictions during the COVID-19 pandemic, however, have had a devastating effect on the economy and food supplies.

Those who are lucky to escape from North Korea often cross to South Korea, which is a free and successful democratic nation.

Communism in Action

Each year, some North Koreans manage to escape their tightly controlled country. Sokeel Park, who works for an organization called Liberty in North Korea (LiNK), interviews these refugees and helps them start new lives in South Korea. Here is what Park said about how they escape from North Korea:

> "Basically, people are dealing with either a frozen river, or trying to wade or swim across a river into China. And obviously, they have to deal with the border security on both sides—there's maybe a couple of ways that people can deal with that. The main way is, actually, through corruption. And there are some people who just take the risk and try to make a run for it—but it's a really desperate measure to take that."

What does this interview tell you about the people of North Korea?

Why do you think they risk leaving the country when the dangers of doing so are so extreme?

CONCLUSION

Communism Past, Present, and Future

Communism started becoming more popular around the world after the Industrial Revolution of the nineteenth century. As a large working class grew, class differences also grew. This working class provided the revolutionary force needed to overthrow the government of Russia, which became the first country under a communist system. Later, other countries staged revolutions and communist leaders took control. Communism reached its peak in the mid-twentieth century, but later declined. Only five countries now have communist political systems.

In China, the main task of the People's Liberation Army (PLA) is to uphold the leadership of the Chinese Communist Party.

A One-Party System

A communist system is a one-party political system, which means only the communist party can be in control of the government. Communist systems have been established through revolutions. Once in power, several communist leaders have also become dictators. A communist economy is a command economy, which means the government sets production goals for its country's industries. The industries produce goods to meet those goals and sell their goods at prices that have been set by the government.

Communism Into the Future

Economies are poor in most communist countries, except for China. Shortages often occur and citizens may not have enough food or goods for their families. They may turn to the black market and pay high prices for the food they need to survive. With such tight controls, many citizens are speaking out for their rights. They want to freely use the Internet and know what government officials are doing. They want the freedom to express their thoughts without fear of being jailed. And with the development of social media, information is reaching more people in a shorter time. With such wide changes, it is not certain whether communism will survive far into the twenty-first century.

Communism in Action

British author Archie Brown wrote the following in his book *The Rise and Fall of Communism*.

> "The idea of building communism, a society in which the state would have withered away, turned out to be a dangerous illusion."

What do you think Archie Brown means by this? Do you agree or disagree with his viewpoint?

How do you think his words can be applied to the communist countries we have looked at around the world in this book?

Political posters in North Korea portray an image of strength and wealth, but can the regime live up to these promises?

Glossary

Bolshevik a member of the Russian Social Democratic party that seized control of the government in the 1917 Revolution in Russia

bourgeoisie the wealthy, property-owning class in a country

capitalism an economic system in which a country's trade and industry are controlled by private owners for profit

censorship to remove sections of a book, movie, or play, or block sites on the Internet that are thought to be harmful or a risk to the public

Cold War the state of hostility that existed between the United States and the USSR, and their allies, between 1945 and 1990

collectives groups made up of a number of people to form new communities

command economy a type of economy that is controlled by a central power and in which factories are publicly owned

communism a system of government in which the state controls all wealth and property

constitution a set of rules and principles that lays down how a nation should be governed

corruption dishonest actions by people in power

cult of personality extreme loyalty to a political leader, usually developed through the use of media and propaganda

dictator a leader who rules with absolute power

elite a group of people with privileges not available to everyone

human rights rights that every human being has, regardless of where they live

intellectual a person who is dedicated to learning and developing thoughts about certain subjects, such a politics or society

Iron Curtain a political and geographical barrier that separated communist and noncommunist countries during the Cold War

legislature the branch of government that debates policy and makes laws

manifesto a written statement declaring the views of its author

Marxist a follower of the political and economic teachings of Karl Marx and Friedrich Engels

peasant a person who works a small farm

philosopher a person who seeks wisdom through study, thought, and discussion

politburo a group of people who oversee the communist party in China

proletariat the urban working class in a country

propaganda the spreading of information to influence public opinion or present a person in a favorable way

revolution a violent upheaval to overthrow a ruler or bring about radical change

sanctions laws that prevent a country from buying goods from or selling them to other countries

socialism an economic system in which land and industries are held by the government, rather than by people

tsar an emperor of Russia

Find Out More

Books

Biohm, Craig E. *Modern Russia: From Revolution to the Invasion of Ukraine.* ReferencePoint Press, 2024.

Hess, Randy K. *Communism* (Control of the State). Mason Crest, 2018.

Uhl, Xina M. *Communism* (Examining Political Systems). Rosen, 2020.

Websites

Find out more about communism at:
https://kids.britannica.com/students/article/communism/273756

Read an overview of communism at:
education.nationalgeographic.org/resource/communism

Some useful videos about the cold war can be found at:
www.neok12.com/Cold-War.htm

Take a closer look at how communism works at:
people.howstuffworks.com/communism.htm

Learn more about the story of communism in this video:
www.youtube.com/watch?v=SM6FGAQOlwM

Publisher's note to educators and parents:
All the websites featured above have been carefully reviewed to ensure that they are suitable for students. However, many websites change often, and we cannot guarantee that a site's future contents will continue to meet our high standards of educational value. Please be advised that students should be closely monitored whenever they access the Internet.

Index

ABOUT THE AUTHOR

Alex Webb has written many children's books and has a particular interest in history and politics. She has found researching and writing this book fascinating and hopes that it helps students everywhere gain knowledge and insight into political systems and how they work.